TRANSFORMING THE LANDSCAPE

Fifty Years on the New RIT Campus

TRANSFORMING THE LANDSCAPE

Fifty Years on the New RIT Campus

Edited by Becky Simmons
Essay by Sarah Thompson

RIT PRESS

Transforming the Landscape: Fifty Years on the New RIT Campus

Published and distributed by:
RIT Press
90 Lomb Memorial Drive
Rochester, New York 14623-5604
http://ritpress.rit.edu

Printed in the U.S.
ISBN 978-1-939125-57-6

Library of Congress Cataloging-in-Publication Data
Names: Rochester Institute of Technology, author. | Simmons, Becky, editor.
Title: Transforming the landscape : fifty years on the new RIT campus / edited by Becky Simmons ; photography edited by Jenn Poggi ; essay by Sarah Thompson.
Description: Rochester, New York : RIT Press, 2018. | Includes bibliographical references.
Identifiers: LCCN 2018018307 | ISBN 9781939125576 (hard cover : alk. paper)
Subjects: LCSH: Rochester Institute of Technology—History. | Rochester Institute of Technology—Planning. | Rochester Institute of Technology—Buildings. | Campus planning—New York (State)—Henrietta (Town) | Henrietta (N.Y. : Town)—Buildings, structures, etc.
Classification: LCC T173.R66 R63 2018 | DDC 378.747/89—dc23
LC record available at https://lccn.loc.gov/2018018307

RIT Campus, looking southwest, 1982

CONTENTS

Josef Albers, *Growth*, in George Eastman Hall, 1979

PRESIDENT'S WELCOME

"Don't get 100 acres. Buy enough land for the next 100 years."

— James Gleason, chairman of the RIT Board of Trustees, 1961

Like so many before me, I was attracted to RIT for many reasons. Prior to my arrival, I had always been aware of RIT's strong reputation, mainly due to my engineering background. I was aware of RIT's leadership in areas such as imaging science and sustainability, and that RIT was home to the National Technical Institute for the Deaf (NTID).

Though born and raised in the Midwest, I was somewhat familiar with Rochester, N.Y. As a child, I was a major consumer of Kodak cameras and film. As a young faculty member at the University of Illinois, I met with research colleagues at Kodak to discuss progress in digital photography, before the advent of the first digital camera.

When I arrived at RIT, I discovered more gems in the arts, design, and humanities. Today, a year later, I remain wide-eyed with a yearning to experience all the different areas of the university. This 50-year celebration of our campus in the town of Henrietta is an opportunity to continue learning about our past and leverage how we can shape the future.

Indeed, RIT's history is fascinating and captivating. This university started with a progressive vision and uncommon ambition. We were born of an unlikely institutional marriage of an influential cultural association, the Rochester Athenaeum, founded in 1829, and a technical training school, the Mechanics Institute, founded in 1885.

The decision to leave downtown Rochester in 1961 for farmland in Henrietta put RIT on its path to preeminence as a global university. Led by Chairman Gleason, the Board of Trustees' bold move allowed President Mark Ellingson to start with a new canvas. This landscape also led to RIT being chosen as the home campus for the federally-sponsored NTID, which also celebrates its 50th anniversary this year.

The modern-day campus flourished at a brisk pace. We are one of the top few universities in the nation working at the intersection of technology, the arts, and design. Today, the university's reputation and reach go well beyond Henrietta and Rochester. We have global partnerships on nearly every continent with campuses located in China, Croatia, Dubai, and Kosovo. We are 125,000 alumni, and Tigers are shaping the future and improving the world.

At RIT, we are transforming the landscape beyond our 15.7 million bricks. There is also an eclectic vibe of personalities. Not everybody has to be the same. In fact, different is good! We have people with blue hair, people with green hair, and of course, orange hair. We're accepting of all, and what really matters are the ideas and the passion that RIT people bring and how they create and innovate. The essence of RIT is our people. Our students, faculty, staff, alumni, and friends will propel this university forward.

This moment in our history is a great time to reflect on how far we have come and also look forward. What's next? Together, we have many more chapters to write in the evolving RIT story. I am convinced that we have covered only the early volumes.

David C. Munson, Jr.
President
RIT

Student Alumni Union, 1979

FOREWORD

Has RIT transformed us, or have we transformed RIT? I believe both are equally true.

In the middle of the 20th century, RIT was already making an indelible mark on higher education, shaping careers for its students, providing the workforce that served as the economic backbone for the Rochester region, and acting as an invaluable partner to companies and industries across the country. In the fifty years since the Henrietta campus began to rise up from fields and wetlands south of the City of Rochester, RIT has expanded its reach and reputation around the globe and deepened its impact on the lives of our students and alumni.

Brick City has become a beacon of knowledge and innovation. The university has been transformed by the leaders, scholars, alumni, and students who have trod the campus pathways. It has altered the trajectory of entire industries and changed the lives of many of its alumni and supporters. It has been embraced by the Rochester community as an integral part of its history and a vital part of its future, and it is heralded by industry, education, and global leaders as a truly great university.

With all that has happened since the grand opening of the new campus in 1968, it is stunning to consider that the transformation is not complete. As we look back on how much has changed since we placed the first brick in Henrietta, the potential for RIT to be transformed and to continue to transform the lives of RIT family members is awe-inspiring.

Our past is being celebrated, but our future awaits.

Bill Buckingham
Honorary Chair of the 50th Anniversary Committee, RIT Board of Trustees member, and RIT Alumnus (MBA, '64)

PREFACE

Transforming the Landscape: Fifty Years on the New RIT Campus is one facet of a yearlong celebration to commemorate the 50th anniversary of Rochester Institute of Technology's Henrietta campus. This anniversary celebration offers the RIT community an opportunity to look back at the university's tremendous growth, due in large part to the bold decision made in 1961 to move the campus from the City of Rochester to 1,300 acres located in suburban Henrietta. The space that RIT gained supported the ensuing growth of the university and allowed for its physical expansion and curricular development. This additional space has taken RIT from a school with six colleges, 49 degree programs, and a handful of master's programs, to a university with 11 colleges and degree granting units, more than 200 programs, 75 master's programs and eight Ph.D. programs, as well as three international campuses.

The downtown campus of RIT, by necessity, grew organically. The campus consisted of some buildings constructed by the school, and others were adapted from their original purpose, including former hotels, homes, and a bakery, all squeezed into a small area. In spite of the space constraint, the staff and students who worked and attended the downtown location remember their concrete campus with affection.

In contrast, the 1968 Henrietta campus was designed conceptually and aesthetically as a whole. After 50 years, the trees have matured, softening the landscape. Careful planning has brought about a place containing varied and beautiful spaces; outdoor rooms for quiet contemplation, study, and play; significant structures; and important artworks.

With a focus on the aesthetic vision for the new campus, the image section of this book was conceived as a visual tour—allowing the reader to enjoy a pictorial journey and to comprehend the growth and development of the new buildings and alterations that have occurred over the past five decades. Integrating historical and contemporary images, the tour begins with the Jefferson Road entrance, moves through the major quadrangles and building areas, and ends with the complex that houses the National Technical Institute for the Deaf.

A project of this scale is due to the contributions of many individuals. Dr. Sarah Thompson, associate professor of architecture in RIT's School of Art, researched and examined archival records related to the construction of the original 1968 campus, teasing out new information for an account of the eight-year journey from empty fields to brick buildings. Her essay tells the story of the people involved in the intricate process of planning and construction, enlightening and offering the reader a new appreciation for RIT's award-winning campus and the importance of its architecture.

Jennifer Poggi, assistant professor of photojournalism in RIT's School of Photographic Arts and Sciences, served as photography editor extraordinaire. Her expertise in editing and sequencing led to the strong visual story communicated in the book. Jody Sidlauskas, associate archivist, and Ella von Holtum, assistant archivist, contributed long hours of image research and review, and prepared the image captions. Their intimate knowledge of RIT history allowed for a thorough understanding of the value of individual images. School of Photographic Arts and Sciences graduate student Gwendolyn Davies spent untold hours scanning and editing images—we owe the quality of the reproductions to her proficiency with scanners and Photoshop.

The professional staff of RIT Press, Molly Cort, Laura DiPonzio Heise, and Marnie Soom, ushered the raw material through to a beautiful book.

RIT Archives holds thousands of images; many were taken by RIT staff. I am especially grateful to the former staff photographers who have meticulously documented the many facets of life at RIT over the last 50 years and whose images grace this book. A special note of appreciation to RIT photographers A. Sue Weisler and Elizabeth Lamark. Their skills with a camera and singular vision are displayed throughout the book. Retired RIT faculty and architectural photographers Bill and Dawn DuBois spent days in Fall 2017 creating a visual record of RIT's campus. Their images, which will form a unique anniversary collection in RIT Archives, capture a specific time and place for future reference bringing a visual timeline to the present. I thank them for their professionalism and enthusiasm for this project.

I am grateful to the members of the 50th Anniversary planning committee for their support of the book. It is my honor to have had this opportunity to make a contribution to the university's anniversary. A final thank you to Dr. Therese Mulligan for her thoughtful assistance with editing the essay and for her steadfast friendship.

New buildings and spaces have been added over the past 50 years. As an RIT employee since 2003, I have been fortunate to witness some of the growth described here. The opportunity to look back to the start of the modern RIT in Henrietta offers the reader an overview of the transformation of the campus accompanied by its history. This book brings home the changes that have taken place since the initial move from downtown Rochester — a physical transformation that ultimately points to the people, programs, projects, and partnerships that make up the institution that is RIT.

Becky Simmons
RIT Archivist

Fig. 1 The Quarter Mile, 1975

BUILDING BRICK CITY

THE DESIGN OF RIT'S HENRIETTA CAMPUS

In November 1962, Rochester Institute of Technology (RIT) contacted multiple architectural firms to negotiate participation in "a responsibility and an opportunity that are extraordinary"[1]: designing and constructing a completely new university campus from the ground up. The hope was to move from RIT's downtown campus at the start of the 1967 academic year, but construction delays pushed completion further into the next year. By fall 1968, when the university transferred all operations to its current home, students were greeted by a new RIT that had very little in common with the typical American university of the time. The campus was arranged following a long central axis, with clustered buildings in bold geometric forms providing education space at one end and living space at the other. (Fig. 1) The visual strength of the buildings was amplified by their deeply recessed windows and entries, and no ornament detracted from their severe contours. Minimalist modern art punctuated courtyards and lobbies. The stylistic historicism of so many institutes of higher learning was nowhere to be found on RIT's new campus, and the site evinced a unity that belied its multiple contributing designers. The Henrietta campus was and remains a branding statement, distinguishing RIT as a determinedly modern technical institution, separating it from its more traditional peers.

The need for a new campus came to the fore in 1959, when the state of New York announced that the extension of the I-490 freeway would likely pass through the heart of RIT's holdings in downtown Rochester. (Fig. 2) When the Athenaeum—the parent institute of what would become RIT—was founded in 1829, it was located in the first iteration of the Reynolds Arcade on Main Street, then in the (now sadly lost) Corinthian Hall on Exchange Place. However, after the merger with the Mechanics Institute in 1891, the urban campus came to be centered in the area roughly bounded by Plymouth, Troup, Clarissa, and Broad streets. RIT did not own all the land or the buildings in the area, resulting in a disjointed but growing urban campus, dotted with buildings whose names would be familiar to RIT students today: the Eastman Building (funded by George Eastman), Nathaniel Rochester Hall (formerly the Hotel Rochester), the George H. Clark Building, Kate Gleason Hall, and Bevier Memorial Building. The state's infrastructure plans seemed poorly timed for RIT, given the Institute's recent investments in construction: the Clark Building dated from 1946; trustee James Gleason announced a $30 million modernization program in late 1951 that would result in new buildings for Graphic Arts and the School for American Craftsmen;[2] the Hotel Rochester had recently been acquired to convert into dormitory space in the mid-1950s; and the Ritter-Clark Memorial Building opened in 1955.

And yet, RIT expected growth beyond what could easily be contained in the constraints of the downtown setting. The GI Bill, the booming post-WWII economy, and rising educational expectations meant larger freshmen classes every year. RIT's enrollment nearly doubled (from 4,376 to 8,546) between 1950 and 1960. The decisions to offer Bachelor of Science degrees beginning in 1955 and to seek Middle States accreditation, granted in 1958, further increased the applicant pool. Students complained about the lack of housing, parking, and communal spaces, problems that would only worsen as the proportion of traditional university students increased in comparison to evening students, who typically were commuters with full-time employment and their own housing. RIT administrators were already debating possibilities for further expansion when the state's announcement coincidentally increased the urgency of the issue and forced a deadline for a decision.

A new campus seemed an easier fiscal solution than trying to secure property rights and work around the planned freeway construction downtown. In the spring of 1960, the RIT administration's questionnaire results showed that RIT students strongly supported moving, while the faculty favored staying. By 1961, Faculty Council had been swayed, and voted 77 to 13 in favor of a move, noting the desire for growth and for a specially designed campus suiting RIT's modern educational needs. The increased desire to leave the downtown campus made RIT part of a broader national trend: though little referenced in archival records of administrative meetings, the increasing perception of the downtown neighborhood as dangerous also weighed on a decision made in an era when many in the northeastern United States who could do so fled industrial cities for nearby suburbs. Were RIT to remain downtown, development would likely be in the then-struggling Third Ward (Corn Hill). The City of Rochester tried encouraging RIT to stay, believing that the neighborhood's revitalization (and associated government funding for neighborhood development) depended on RIT's presence. A few faculty members did voice concerns about the fate of the district they would leave behind. Meanwhile, a quiet search for a potential new location eventually yielded a site in Henrietta via an RIT alumnus, Emil Muller, and in 1961 RIT acquired options on

Fig. 2 President Mark Ellingson (left) and Senator Kenneth B. Keating with diagram indicating proposed highway through campus, 1963

1,300 acres some six miles south of the existing campus.

The Daily Record, a local newspaper targeting the business and real estate communities, reported in August of 1961 that RIT was still considering two proposals—a move to Henrietta or a downtown expansion. But RIT administrators had been discussing more specific plans for a new campus with a consultant in April of that year, with meeting notes reflecting some of the broad ideas later adopted in the campus layout: the separation of academic and living spaces, a central library, recreation and communal spaces at the perimeter, and "interesting open spatial relationships."[3] The Board of Trustees made the decision public with a vote on November 20, 1961: RIT would indeed have a new campus in Henrietta. A letter of December 21, 1961, from RIT president Mark Ellingson thanked Henrietta Town Supervisor Don W. Cook, stating that RIT was moving to what would likely be the center of the metropolitan area in years to come and presciently suggesting enrollment would double or even triple.[4]

PLANNING THE NEW CAMPUS

Ellingson presided over the most significant changes in RIT's history to date: the adoption of the name Rochester Institute of Technology in 1944; the move to awarding bachelor's and master's degrees; the arrival of various schools and programs that would become the School of Media Sciences, the School

Fig. 3 Aileen Osborn Webb with coordinating architect Lawrence Anderson to her right, 1963

for American Crafts, and the Saunders College of Business; the establishment of the National Technical Institute for the Deaf; and of course the move to the Henrietta site. His interest in the new campus seems to have been strongly connected to ideas of functionality and future growth. He laid out his "basic philosophical thinking"[5] in a January 1962 trustee meeting, and ideas of economy and practicality that were stressed to the media seem to have originated with him. Much of the credit for the aesthetic considerations of the campus should go to longtime RIT trustee Aileen Osborn Webb. Aileen Webb came from and married into substantial wealth and devoted her life to the support of craft and craft education, founding the American Craft Council, the School for American Craftsmen (which moved to RIT in 1950 and is now the School for American Crafts), the Museum of Contemporary Craft (now the Museum of Arts and Design) in New York City, and the World Craft Council. She had an enduring friendship with Ellingson and was tapped quite early to be a voice—likely the strongest voice—in the new campus design. In an oral history interview in 1992 for the Smithsonian's Archives of American Art, architect Lawrence Anderson, who was the consulting architect for the new RIT campus, remembered Webb as having influenced the process "very greatly": "And she was, of course, very aware of the New York scene and the architectural world and wanted to get good talent, as much of it as possible."[6] (Fig. 3)

Webb served as the vice chair of the Building Committee and initiated early steps in the planning process. Within ten days of the public announcement about the move, Webb suggested hiring modern landscape designer Daniel Urban Kiley, who had recently worked on the new United States Air Force Academy as a site architect, and he was invited to RIT the following January.[7] Meeting notes from March 1962 indicate that she encouraged Ellingson and RIT planning director F. Dow Hamblin to educate themselves with photographs of the work of potential architects.[8] However, in a June meeting, the Building Committee put off stylistic choices until the general arrangement and site plan had been determined. In July of 1962, the president of Webb's American Craftsmen's Council, David Campbell, began serving as a consultant on the new campus project.[9] In early August 1962, at a Vermont retreat, the Building Committee decided that the design responsibility for the new campus would be parceled out among multiple architects. The committee then created a new committee, the Design, Planning, and Construction Committee, to manage all of the design-related elements of the complex enterprise ahead. Webb chaired the new committee, comprised of Donald McMaster (RIT trustee and chair of the Building Committee), Molly Stern (wife of the chairman of the Board of Trustees, Arthur Stern), F. Dow Hamblin, David Campbell (already hired as an education consultant), Dan Kiley, and Nelson Tower (engineering consultant). Webb hosted their first meeting in New York City later that month, where they winnowed down a list of architects. The committee wanted to employ a top consulting architect as a kind of primary manager, and they added Lawrence Anderson, who at the time directed the MIT architecture program (he would later become Dean of MIT's School of Architecture and Planning), to the design committee. At a meeting at RIT in September, the members compiled a list of architects' names including Harry Weese, Hugh Stubbins, Kevin Roche, and Edward Barnes—the four who would later be selected along with Anderson and Kiley—as well as figures such as I.M. Pei and Marcel Breuer. (Fig. 4)

From the beginning, every designer of interest to the RIT administration was an established and dedicated

Fig. 4 Architects with model of future RIT campus, 1963

modernist. RIT's commitment to a modern design was made with minimal discussion, notable given the relatively recent acceptance of a modern aesthetic for university architecture; American universities did not fully embrace modernism until after World War II. Through the 1930s, most campus designs or campus expansions relied on historicizing architectural forms. Gothic Revival, which associated American institutions with medieval European university foundations (and often used quadrangular layouts derived from the cloisters of monastic forebears), and Beaux-Arts were particularly prevalent from the last decade of the 19th century through the first decades of the 20th. Most institutions of higher education wanted the impression of endurance and prestige associated with historical styles. Even when the industrial materials commonly used by modern architects made an appearance, they often still wore costumes: consider the Cathedral of Learning, a steel-framed Gothic Revival skyscraper on the campus of the University of Pittsburgh.

The post-WWII higher education boom created opportunities for new directions in campus design: new institutions were founded; existing sites needed to grow; and universities began to expand their services and offerings, requiring new types of campus buildings. However, the use of modern architectural forms was not universally welcomed, even after the war. In October 1949, former Bauhaus director (and at the time, professor at Harvard's Graduate School of Design) Walter Gropius published "Not Gothic but Modern for Our Colleges" in the *New York Times*, indicating that a leading voice in the field still felt it was necessary to make the argument for "a new code of visual values" that put aside historical disguise.[10]

While some 200 new campuses were underway in 1962,[11] only a very few modern campuses had been completed at the time when the Henrietta campus was planned, putting RIT in the vanguard. The downtown campus had already established that, given the opportunity to build rather than convert existing structures, RIT was unusual among its peers in opting for modern, functional forms. The industrial brick of the downtown Eastman Building (since demolished), the naturally derived geometric patterns of Claude Bragdon's polychrome tile on the Bevier Memorial Building, and the Streamline Moderne of the Clark Building (altered and reclad to become the Rochester City School District administration building) all testified to a turn from historicism and a willingness to place innovation over tradition. What could that willingness to embrace modernism look like when applied holistically to a campus plan?

Frank Lloyd Wright's Florida Southern College, begun in 1938, is one of only a handful of prewar examples of modern campus design. Illinois Institute of Technology's (IIT) new campus, masterminded by Mies van der Rohe after his arrival at IIT in 1938, was likely a stronger influence on RIT, as it demonstrated a marriage of the dedicated technical institution with geometric planning, minimalist design, and an emphasis on modern, industrially produced materials. (Fig. 5) Other examples of the modern campus available to planners at RIT included Walter Gropius and Marcel Breuer's work for Black Mountain College in the 1940s, executed by A. Lawrence Kocher; Eliel and Eero Saarinen at Drake University in the late 1940s and 1950s; Walter Netsch's work as lead architect for Skidmore, Owings & Merrill at the Air Force Academy in the late 1950s; Paul Rudolph's plan for the Tuskegee Institute, commissioned in 1958; and William Pereira's plan for the University of California at Irvine, and Edward Durell Stone's design for SUNY Albany, both launched in the early 1960s. The presence of Breuer on

Fig. 5 Crown Hall, Illinois Institute of Technology, 1960s

the RIT shortlist, the interest in Kevin Roche, who worked with Saarinen and would eventually take over Saarinen's office, and the selection of site planner Dan Kiley, fresh from his work at the Air Force Academy, indicate that the design committee was taking note of emerging trends in university architecture.

By October 1962, the design committee experienced some friction over fiscal priorities versus design priorities. Nelson Tower of Tower and Wood, the firm that would oversee the engineering aspects of campus construction, created a list of desirable qualities for potential architects: they should be experienced with campus planning, have a strong eye for functionality, should be able to give personal attention to the RIT campus, and should demonstrate an ability to follow a budget. Tower's practicality was apparently met with resistance by his fellow design committee members. Arthur Stern's letter of October 19, 1962, conveyed conversations with Webb, his fellow trustee, to Ellingson, and politely requested that Ellingson ask Hamblin (the planning director) and the engineers on the design committee to refrain from attending meetings where architects were discussed, as they were concerned with finances and execution, not planning.[12] Webb, firmly on the side of aesthetics, would later write to Ellingson about the dispute, stating that the committee desired "as fine a group of buildings as possible to meet the Institute's needs, not monumental buildings but ones expressive of our times, functional, and beautiful." She argued for the consideration of more than cost; if they considered design impact, they could "maintain [RIT] on a level with the other great technical institutes of our country."[13]

SELECTING THE ARCHITECTS

The committee began to solicit participation from its final choices in November. In a letter on behalf of the Building Committee dated November 1, 1962, to Harry Weese Associates, the basics of the project were established, and Tower's practical concerns are still present, but are married with aesthetic aspirations. The Building Committee wanted five or six architectural firms to work together; the general plan would have educational buildings and dormitories as two hubs on high ground, connected by a dike. "What kind of campus is envisioned by the committee?" The authors seemingly have no pretensions: "...this will be an economy campus. RIT is not a candidate for membership in the Ivy League." The committee stressed that RIT was an institution that emphasized hard work, experiential learning, and accessibility to all "without consideration of economic background. Academic buildings will be rugged but simple. The range of materials and construction techniques and finishes must necessarily be limited, and beauty must come through quality of space and proportion and a sense of ordered form." Regardless of the need to keep costs manageable, the committee felt the project was a high calling: "This new installation ought to be...a leading example among technical institutes, and an inspiring environment for living and work in the university tradition. We believe this goal can be achieved without undue emphasis on innovation, originality, personality, and melodrama. We prefer sensitivity, sensibility, humility, ingenuity, and restraint."[14] Similar letters went out to Hugh Stubbins and Associates, Kevin Roche (who transformed Saarinen's practice into Kevin Roche John Dinkeloo and Associates as the RIT project progressed), and Edward Larrabee Barnes Associates. All four accepted the offer.

Each architect involved with the 1968 campus had an educational background that brought him into contact with iconic figures of modern design, each established a substantial practice prior to working at RIT, and all focused on commercial and institutional architecture, most with significant experience in designing for a university setting. Dan Kiley was the landscape architect for such sites as the Dallas Museum of Art and Philadelphia's Independence Mall in addition to designing the grounds at the Air Force Academy.

Lawrence Anderson, a partner in Anderson, Beckwith, and Haible, chaired the MIT architecture program and designed multiple buildings at MIT, as well as additions at the University of Virginia, Boston University, and Rutgers University.

Hugh Stubbins and Associates was a Massachusetts firm; Stubbins had assisted Walter Gropius at Harvard and eventually chaired the architecture department there. His career encompassed the Kongresshalle in Berlin; multiple buildings for Harvard, Princeton, and Hampshire College; dormitories at Mount Holyoke; dormitories at the University of Massachusetts Amherst; the Senior Center at Bowdoin; College Five (now Porter College) at the University of California at Santa Cruz; the Citigroup Center; additions to the Museum of Fine Arts, Boston; and later on, the Ronald Reagan Presidential Library.

Harry Weese Associates was based in Chicago. Weese had studied at MIT and Yale, and had held a fellowship at the Cranbrook Academy of Art before briefly joining Skidmore, Owings & Merrill. He became well known for work in a university setting, counting the University of Illinois, the University of Chicago, the University of Wisconsin, Cornell College (IA), and MIT among his clients; he was also responsible for Chicago's Time–Life building and for the design of Washington's Metro stations.

Kevin Roche John Dinkeloo and Associates had a Connecticut base, and both principals had worked extensively with Eero Saarinen, completing such famed projects as the Gateway Arch in St. Louis and the TWA terminal in New York City. Roche had studied at IIT with Mies van der Rohe and would go on to design the Oakland Museum, the Ford Foundation headquarters, the Fine Arts Building at the University of Massachusetts Amherst, United Nations Plaza I and II, and the Lehman Pavilion of the Metropolitan Museum of Art. He won the Pritzker Architecture Prize in 1982.

Edward Larrabee Barnes, a Harvard graduate, had studied with Gropius and Breuer. After his work at RIT, he would go on to design the Dallas Museum of Art, the Walker Arts Center, the IBM Building, and the master plans for SUNY Purchase and SUNY Potsdam.

A COLLABORATIVE EFFORT

At a New York City meeting held November 13 and 14, 1962, the architects divided responsibility according to specific campus quadrants: Roche and Dinkeloo oversaw communal spaces, including the College Union, gym, and ice rink, as well as George Eastman Hall; Weese worked on the library and the General Studies building; Stubbins would design the Graphic Arts and Photography and Fine and Applied Arts buildings; Anderson would work on the Science and Applied Science buildings; and Barnes would handle the dormitories of Sol Heumann Hall, Nathaniel Rochester Hall, Kate Gleason Hall, and Grace Watson Hall. Each firm would ultimately work with two deans related to their architectural charges. The apartments planned for married student housing, located at some distance from the campus's residential hub, went unassigned and were eventually designed by Corgan and Balestiere, a Rochester-based firm.

To economize, encourage collaboration, and minimize redundancy, the group agreed to be paid based on set professional fees rather than on a percentage of building costs. They began to work on a site plan that would fulfill the general specifications of two hubs connected by a causeway, based not only on optimal site conditions but also on the notion that resident students should have dedicated living and leisure space away from their working space, particularly important because RIT's large population of evening commuter students kept academic buildings busy at night.

The first full meeting of the design committee and all the architects took place in January of 1963, and planning continued throughout the year, with multiple visits by the architects to the Henrietta site. Each college provided space and growth estimates, detailing specific kinds of rooms and needs for their programs. The Fine and Applied Arts faculty seem to have been the only faculty members to share an aesthetic concern in response to a space survey: they specified a desire that the exterior of their building should reflect the design emphasis and function within. Surveying, planning, and editing plans occupied most of the year, and it wasn't until May 1964 that information on grading the site was sent out to contractors. The first construction contract was signed in fall of 1964, and the ground was broken for George Eastman Hall and Liberal Arts Hall soon after.

Financial issues, labor, planning, and weather all slowed the pace of construction. Roche reworked his initial plan for George Eastman Hall between 1963 and 1964: whereas most of the architects had followed Henrietta's restrictions on building height, Roche felt that the campus required a visual anchor to parallel Barnes's dormitory blocks. Both the Federal Aviation Agency and the Town of Henrietta had to allow for code exceptions—Henrietta prohibited construction over 35 feet in height—and these were granted in July 1964.[15] A number of the colleges were told to revise their space estimates in order to trim the budget. Hamblin kept monthly records and reported in July of 1965 that the architects were slow to agree on a plan and on definitive building forms, which then pushed back the bidding timeline. He also noted that four of the seven academic buildings were over budget. Barnes, in particular, was regularly scolded for delays in providing the dormitory plans. Dan Kiley was dismissed by RIT in May of 1966, following a dispute in which Kiley countered RIT's claims about going over budget by stating that RIT's administrators did not comprehend the complexity of their project or their requests. Webb diplomatically objected to his dismissal, but was not able to repair the relationship, and the landscape design envisioned by Kiley was never fully executed. By July of 1966, the engineering firm Wood and Tower issued a memo to all the architecture firms declaring that no further cost overruns would be approved unless absolutely essential. The overruns and delays meant that the campus missed its 1967 completion target date.

THE NEW CAMPUS OPENS

When the campus opened the following year, the academic side contained more than a million square feet of floor space spread over 13 buildings. The causeway connecting the academic and residential sides on the two areas of high ground was transformed by the architects into the campus's organizing axis, now known as the Quarter Mile. RIT's designers remained traditional in terms of planning, working with

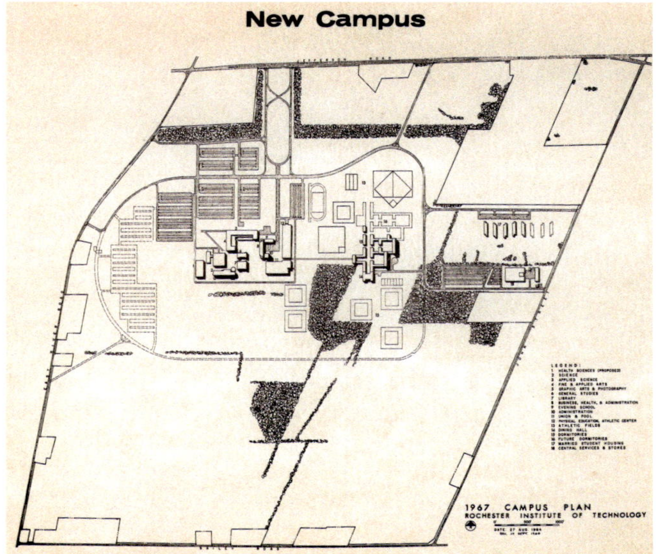

Fig. 6 New campus plan, 1967

a directional, inward-facing layout and buildings meeting at right angles rather than the more organic, curvilinear or clustered patterns coming into use in campus planning of the 1950s. (Fig. 6)

The buildings themselves were sculptural and determinedly modern. The tall, staggered rectangles of Barnes's dormitories anchored one end of the axis. The spacing between Roche's gym and College Union (now the Student Alumni Union, or SAU) buildings created a narrow portal between two steep, sheer brick wall surfaces, meaning that students approaching from the dorms had a sense of entering a fortress or citadel; only the George Eastman Hall tower broke the horizontal line of the silhouette. The sharp angle of the SAU, cut away at ground level so as not to interrupt the axis, (Fig. 7) creates a courtyard protecting a recessed entry, which opens to a steel-and-glass-covered atrium. The triangular skylights, echoing the form of the projection housing Ingle Auditorium, seem to be set on top of the brick, the thinness and transparency of the glass accentuating the brick's mass.

Roche and Dinkeloo's Eastman complex, conceived as three rectangles forming the sides of a quadrangle, uses gridded fenestration, the regular, deep-set placement of

Fig. 7 Student Alumni Union, 1972

Fig. 8 George Eastman Hall, 1978

the windows exposing the strength of the brick. The wider windows at the corners of the tower emphasize the bilateral symmetry of its facade. (Fig. 8) Weese's General Studies Building (Liberal Arts Hall) and library face each other across the main axis; Weese aligned them to create a minor axis, and their strongly buttressed corners and horizontal planes mirror each other. The Graphic Arts and Photography and Fine and Applied Arts (GAP-FAA) buildings, now the Frank E. Gannett and James E. Booth buildings, were built into a slope; Stubbins created deeply sheltered access points at both the second and first floors to account for changes in elevation. The two buildings read as a series of stacked planar volumes, with the central floors cantilevered outward and the upper levels receding. Anderson's Science and Applied Science buildings (now Thomas Gosnell Hall and James E. Gleason Hall), visually connected by porticoes at ground level, create a courtyard—since named the Infinity Quad after José de Rivera's *Construction #105* in the center—terminating what was then the far western end of the campus's central axis.

The choice of brick as the primary exterior material—the 1968 campus incorporated more than six million—unified the buildings and complemented their geometric forms. The brick pathways directly connected the experience of buildings and landscape, but years later were replaced with concrete and pavers when it became clear they could not stand up to Rochester weather. The architects made the most of the brick, using it to create broad, flat wall spans and precise reveals. While heavy massing, exposure of materials, and minimalist ornament associate RIT with the architectural style known as Brutalism, (Fig. 9) the brick's color creates warmth, texture, and variegated color in contrast to the concrete (*béton brut*) more typically seen in Brutalist works. The weight, solidity, and textured surfaces of the brick remove RIT from the International Style of Mies van der Rohe at IIT and relate the campus to the works of figures such as Saarinen or Louis Kahn, who had completed the brick First Unitarian Church in Rochester in 1962. The actual brick, Belden ironspot, was a suggestion of Kevin Roche[16] and has become a campus trademark; Belden sells it only to RIT.

The buildings were further connected by the architects' shared vocabulary. Each created a play of fundamental geometric solids and voids, as in the cutout corners of the Gleason building and the deep cutaways on the ground floor of the Eastman tower. The solid weight of the buildings was emphasized by the use of deep setbacks and fortress-like embrasures that revealed the thickness of the walls and created heavy rectangular shadows. The clean forms,

Fig. 9 Thomas Gosnell Hall, 1972

right-angled organization, exposed materials, and lack of applied ornament implied an honesty of expression, and the architects used external forms to refer to interior arrangements. All the buildings have external fenestration aligning with internal floor levels, and Weese's and Stubbins's contributions highlight external floor levels with steel edging to further express their internal plans. Liberal Arts Hall rests on two low, wide cylinders that refer to the shape of the rooms inside, with the vertical placement of the brick differentiating these forms from the horizontal levels above. The result of the architectural collaboration—strong, sculptural, functional, rational—encapsulated the essence of RIT as a modern university.

ART AS PUNCTUATION

Two percent of the construction budget was reserved for art, and the choices were conceived almost as architectural sculpture, with the aim of articulating the new spaces of the RIT campus. Aileen Webb, Arthur Stern, and Molly Stern negotiated the acquisitions, and in accordance with their tastes, the artists represented were well known for their abstract, minimalist work; all worked in media represented in RIT's programs in the Fine and Applied Arts college. Several, including William Keyser and the Bauhaus-trained Frans Wildenhain, were professors within the School for American Crafts.

The ends of the Quarter Mile were marked on the east with Alistair Bevington's enormous *Sundial* and on the west with Jose de Rivera's *Construction #105*. Though polished while *Sundial* has oxidized, *Construction #105* also interacts with the space surrounding it, turning slowly throughout the day. Henry Moore's bronze, *Reclining Figure No. 1,* creates a textural, organic contrast with its angular surroundings, gesturing toward the human form.

Art works installed indoors accentuated architectural functions, as with woodworker and furniture designer William Keyser's elegant window screen (no longer extant), which filtered light through registers of thin diagonals. Murals and tapestries stretched over wall surfaces: *Allegory of a Landscape*, Frans Wildenhain's ceramic mural for the lobby of Ingle Auditorium, echoes the color of the brick but turns the joints into the boundaries of plots of land, creating the effect of an aerial view of the abstracted Finger Lakes countryside. *Grand Hieroglyph*, a tapestry by Sheila Hicks now in the George Eastman Hall tower, varies woven effects to create a richly textured monochrome surface. Ragnhild Langlet's *Blue and White Tapestry* (now in storage) brought linear detail to the SAU dining hall. Harry Bertoia designed three bronze planters with rough surfaces directly evoking the processes of modeling and casting (now in the lobby of Golisano Hall). RIT would soon receive a number of Bertoia's works as a gift from Eastman Kodak Company, including the dandelion sculptures he designed for Kodak's World's Fair pavilion in 1964.

The participation of Josef Albers in the design of site-specific works for RIT was a particular triumph. Albers' work informed a generation of American modernists. His academic affiliations, first at the Bauhaus, and later at Black Mountain College and Yale, made him a model for the artist-as-educator, and his abstract explorations of color, composition, and texture were an ideal complement to RIT's minimalism. Albers created three works for the new campus: he turned an external wall of Gosnell into a patterned mural exploring the possibilities of brick shape and placement, and he painted two murals, *Growth* and *Youth*, for the lobby of George Eastman Hall. *Growth* and *Youth*, each 18' x 18', face each other across the lobby and draw from Albers' *Homage to the Square* series. His repeated drawings, prints, and paintings of nested squares explored the interaction of juxtaposed colors within precisely defined boundaries. The examples at RIT, with squares in deepening shades of yellow-orange, are the only murals in the series.

REACTIONS

At the time of move-in in 1968, students and faculty alike were struck by a campus like none they had ever seen before. During those first years, the campus seemed less than welcoming, isolated from the familiar and compact surroundings of downtown, with incomplete walkways and minimal landscaping. (Fig. 10) It took time to settle into new spaces and establish new workday patterns. Communal areas within the main academic buildings had been reduced for the sake of economy, so there were few places to socialize or collaborate indoors between classes. Students complained about the effects of wind and weather, about maintenance problems in the dorms, and about the campus's perceived coldness and rigidity; at times it did not seem designed with human users at the forefront. Designer Ronald Beckman, visiting in 1975, felt the campus was excessively monumental, even oppressive, and referred to the campus as "Mussolini modern."[17]

In retrospect, the architects had mixed feelings about the success of the project. Interviewed by *The Architectural Record* in 1968, Roche opined that a single firm should have managed the overall planning. While Weese and Anderson felt the collaboration worked, all the participants found the design process difficult at times, and Anderson would later recall being particularly bothered by the budget issues. The architects commented similarly on the effects of financial restraints on interiors and landscaping. However, the architectural establishment felt that these were minor detractions from a groundbreaking achievement. In 1972, RIT's campus design received an American Institute of Architects award for Collaborative Achievement in Architecture, an honor previously bestowed only twice: for the Seagram building and plaza in New York and for San Francisco's Ghirardelli Square. The New York State Association of Architects recognized RIT's achievement the same year, specifically noting the successful execution of a controversial design.

Fig. 10 Infinity Quad, ca. 1968

THE CAMPUS GROWS

RIT's continued expansion—in enrollment, faculty, administration, services, programs, and research—meant that the 1968 campus changed relatively quickly. In response to criticism about the harshness of the new site, campus planners began to address the issue of landscaping in the early 1970s, altering some of the initial pathways to create more organic connections between buildings. With attention to natural groupings of plants and trees, and with time to mature, RIT's landscape has softened the sharpness of the campus's original design and blunted the worst effects of wind, making the environment substantially more welcoming. The Tojo Meditation Garden, a Japanese garden memorializing RIT photography student Yasuji Tojo, was added to the Eastman Kodak Quad in front of Frank E. Gannett Hall in 1975, and its organic lines contrast with the geometric buildings on all sides.

The early seventies also saw the arrival of new buildings for the National Technical Institute for the Deaf. NTID was established by federal law in 1965, but RIT was not officially chosen as the site for the school until 1966, when the planning for the Henrietta campus was already complete. Hugh Stubbins designed NTID's initial buildings, a decision made while he was still at work on the core campus, and he brought the same sensibility he used for Booth and Gannett to Lyndon Baines Johnson Hall.

The original design charge for the Henrietta campus asked the architects to accommodate growth, but the 1968 campus actually proved difficult to expand in a cohesive way, largely because of the sloping, marshy landscape: the designers had used the acreage most suited to construction, and the inward-facing buildings of the academic sector meant that designers of additions had literally an uphill battle trying to connect standing structures and new projects. Furthermore, the nature of additions over time meant that each new building would be a product of its specific circumstances rather than be built as an organic part of the original concept. After Stubbins's work for NTID, the next major projects were Max Lowenthal Hall, built in the late 1970s, and additions to the SAU (Monroe Hall and the Schmitt Interfaith Center). The firm of Macon and Chaintreuil handled these commissions, as well as the Welcome Center in 1978, the Bausch and Lomb Center later in the 1980s, an addition to Wallace Library in 1991, and the Hale-Andrews Student Life Center in 1991. Macon and Chaintreuil produced buildings that respected the forms of the 1968 campus but expanded their vocabulary, as with the concrete transverse arcade in front of the Bausch and Lomb Center or the visible wood of the Schmitt Interfaith Center's interior. Engineering Hall and the Chester F. Carlson Center for Imaging Science were added in the late 1980s. Macon and Chaintreuil evolved into MCJS architects (now CJS), completing Golisano Hall in 2003, a substantial addition to the Gleason building in 2007, and the University Services Center and Student Innovation Hall in 2009.

SWBR Architects also left a substantial mark on the RIT campus, designing Louise Slaughter Hall, Engineering Technology Hall, Sustainability Institute Hall, and Magic Spell Studios. HBT Architects designed Rosica Hall in 2013, as well as the College of Health Sciences and Technology addition to Slaughter Hall in 2015. Other additions since 2000 include the Gordon Field House (Cannon Design, 2004), The Center for Bioscience Education and Technology (EYP Architecture and Engineering, 2007), Global Village (ARC/Architectural Resources Cambridge, 2009), the Vignelli Center for Design Studies (Massimo Vignelli, 2010), Institute Hall (Bergmann Associates, 2012), and the Gene Polisseni Center (Brisbin Brook Beynon, 2014).

The mandated incorporation of ironspot brick into all new structures helps maintain some level of consistency, although the bricks' color shifted slightly in the 1970s when Belden ended coal-fired production. The newer buildings also maintain the interest in geometric form, though the depth of setbacks and recesses decreased substantially after the 1980s. Several newer buildings display dynamic interior spaces absent from the original campus. This is evidenced in the double-height brick and concrete lobby of Lowenthal with its exposed staircase, and in the striking full-height atrium of Sustainability Institute Hall, where transparent materials used for lecture halls, laboratories, and study rooms open the space and the green wall brings the landscape indoors. The mass of the 1968 architecture lightens in newer construction; one can almost date buildings by the amount of glass incorporated. In the Vignelli Center, a gridded glass curtain wall evokes the midcentury aesthetic of the Booth building behind it; in Sustainability Institute Hall, the glass is bookended with brick and topped with a winged roof raised on Corbusian *pilotis*, and the glass is an appropriate complement. In others, the glass expanses speak to a generic technical architecture that could be found at any number of universities. Institute Hall, which incorporates an illuminated RIT logo above its curved glass curtain wall, makes the connection between high-tech modern architecture and the RIT brand explicit. Changes are not purely driven by taste: architects have access to improved materials; new buildings need to meet new functions not anticipated on the 1968 campus; and RIT now has an impressive number of Leadership in Energy and Environmental Design (LEED)-certified buildings. It has earned this designation, established by the U.S. Green Buildings Council, six times over to date, and set a standard that all new RIT construction will, at a minimum, meet LEED silver requirements. This speaks to RIT's commitment to sustainability. Features such as windmills, solar panels, and green roofs make this commitment a featured part of campus design.

As the west side of campus expanded, it was no longer practical to maintain the central axis, and Campus Planning and Design has worked to develop secondary axes, paved walkways, and incorporate plantings to emphasize that the additions all belong to the same space. Additions such as Global Village add density rather than sprawl. As RIT edges toward an enrollment of 20,000, there comes a point when more acreage makes crossing campus between classes less practical.

Even with the criticism of the 1970s (and still today—RIT regularly makes lists of least beautiful campuses, as it did in the 2017 *Princeton Review*),[18] RIT's collaborative campus plan achieved a rare harmony of design, which is remarkable given the scale and complexity of the endeavor. In 1968, the striking contrast between the stark modernity of the RIT campus and the architecture of a typical American university marked RIT as an innovative, dynamic institution set apart from its more traditional peers. Subsequent additions and alterations have enhanced the functionality of the campus and made it more visually welcoming and physically navigable, though they have also diluted the impact of the original designers' bold concept. Expanded planes of gridded glass and steel in more recent structures convey RIT's investment in modern technology, but the forms and materials of the new buildings are less expressive of a specific RIT identity: they are practical and contemporary, but more generic than the singular statement of the 1968 plan. The RIT brick remains, however, and ties current construction to the mid-century campus design. Fifty years later, we pause to examine the context of the campus's creation, and to celebrate the ingenuity and optimism of those who made that creation possible.

Sarah Thompson
Associate Professor, School of Art
College of Art and Design

NOTES

1 Donald McMaster to Harry Weese, November 1, 1962, Box 2, Folder 5, President's Records on Henrietta Campus Construction, RIT Archives.

2 Al Booth, "RIT Board OKs Mammoth Expansion: Modernization Program Costing $30 Million Set," *RIT Reporter*, November 16, 1951.

3 David Campbell, Notes, April 20, 1961, Box 1, Folder 7, President's Records on Henrietta Campus Planning Documents, RIT Archives.

4 Mark Ellingson to Don Cook, December 21, 1961, Box 1, Folder 1, President's Records on Construction of RIT's Henrietta Campus Documents, RIT Archives.

5 Building Committee meeting minutes, January 4, 1962, Box 2, Folder 5, President's Records on Henrietta Campus Construction, RIT Archives.

6 Robert F. Brown, "Oral History Interview with Lawrence Anderson, January 30 – March 30, 1992," transcript, Smithsonian Archives of American Art, accessed September 3, 2017. https://www.aaa.si.edu/collections/interviews/oral-history-interview-lawrence-anderson-12388.

7 Mark Ellingson to Frank Benz, November 30, 1961, Box 1, Folder 4, President's Records on Henrietta Campus Construction, RIT Archives.

8 Mark Ellingson to F. Dow Hamblin, March 5, 1962, Box 2, Folder 5, President's Records on Henrietta Campus Construction, RIT Archives.

9 David Campbell to Mark Ellingson, January 18, 1962, Box 1, Folder 2, President's Records on Henrietta Campus Construction, RIT Archives. Campbell passed away in early 1963.

10 Walter Gropius, "Not Gothic but Modern for Our Colleges," *New York Times Magazine*, October 23, 1949.

11 Paul Venable Turner, *Campus: An American Planning Tradition* (Cambridge, MA: MIT Press, 1995), 249.

12 Arthur Stern to Mark Ellingson, October 19, 1962, Box 1, Folder 7, President's Records on Henrietta Campus Construction, RIT Archives.

13 Aileen Webb to Mark Ellingson, December 15, 1962, Box 1, Folder 7, President's Records on Henrietta Campus Construction, RIT Archives.

14 Donald McMaster to Harry Weese, November 1, 1962, Box 2, Folder 5, President's Records on Henrietta Campus Construction, RIT Archives.

15 F. Dow Hamblin, Campus History, Ch. 17, p. 2, Box 2, Folder 1, President's Records on Construction of RIT's Henrietta Campus Documents, RIT Archives.

16 Vilma Barr, "Team Approach for a Unified Result," *American Institute of Architects Journal*, April 1972, 47.

17 "The Angry Man of Architecture," *Rochester Times-Union*, February 28, 1975.

18 "Least Beautiful Campus," *Princeton Review*, accessed November 27, 2017, https://www.princetonreview.com/college-rankings?rankings=least-beautiful-campus.

BIBLIOGRAPHY

Archival Sources

Holdings of the RIT Archives, including Construction of RIT's Henrietta Campus Records, RIT Henrietta Campus Maps, and RIT President's Records on Henrietta Campus Construction

Published Sources

"The Angry Man of Architecture." *Rochester Times-Union*, February 28, 1975.

Barr, Vilma. "Team Approach for a Unified Result." *American Institute of Architects Journal*, April 1972, 46–50.

Booth, Al. "RIT Board OKs Mammoth Expansion: Modernization Program Costing $30 Million Set." *RIT Reporter*, November 16, 1951.

Brown, Robert F. "Oral History Interview with Lawrence Anderson, January 30 – March 30, 1992." Smithsonian Archives of American Art. Accessed September 3, 2017. https://www.aaa.si.edu/collections/interviews/oral-history-interview-lawrence-anderson-12388.

"Building Consultants Aid in New Campus Designs." *RIT Reporter*, December 7, 1962.

"The Campus: Architecture's Show Place." *Time*, September 21, 1970, 76–82.

"Campus Designed by Co-Operation." *Architectural Record*, June 1965, 162–66.

Chapman, M. Perry. *American Places: In Search of the Twenty-First Century Campus*. American Council on Education/Praeger Series on Higher Education. Westport, CT: Praeger Publishers, 2006.

"A College Arts Complex Shaped by a Strong Master Plan." *Architectural Record*, April 1971, 93–99.

Gaines, Thomas A. *The Campus as a Work of Art*. New York: Praeger Publishers, 1991.

Gordon, Dane R. *Rochester Institute of Technology: Industrial Development and Educational Innovation in an American City*. 2d ed. Rochester, NY: RIT Press, 2007.

Mayer, Frederick W. *A Setting for Excellence: The Story of the Planning and Development of the Ann Arbor Campus of the University of Michigan*. Ann Arbor: University of Michigan Press, 2015.

Schmertz, Mildred F. "RIT's New Campus: A Unique Design Collaboration." *Architectural Record*, November 1968, 123–34.

Simmons, Becky, Houghton Wetherald, David Pankow, and Cary Graphic Arts Press, eds. *View It!: The Art and Architecture of RIT*. 1st ed. Rochester, NY: RIT Cary Graphic Arts Press, 2004.

Turner, Paul Venable. *Campus: An American Planning Tradition*. 2nd ed. Architectural History Foundation Books. New York : Cambridge, Mass: Architectural History Foundation; MIT Press, 1995.

OF TECHNOLOGY

DOWNTOWN

RIT campus, intersection of Broad Street and Washington Street, ca. 1947

Manual Training Building, RIT's first building, erected in 1894, ca. 1895

Class of 1916 poses on steps of Bevier Memorial Building, 1916

(Left) First Presbyterian Church, known as the RIT Chapel, ca. 1950s
(Top right) Eastman Building, ca. 1913
(Bottom right) Kate Gleason Hall, ca. 1965

(Top left) RIT City Center, ca. 1960s
(Top right) Ritter-Clark Memorial Gymnasium and Ice Rink, ca. 1960s
(Bottom left) Bevier Memorial Building, ca. 1965
(Bottom right) School for American Craftsmen, ca. 1960s

WE'RE COMING, HENRIETTA!

RIT Reporter

SEE YOU IN 196?

OFFICIAL PUBLICATION OF THE ROCHESTER INSTITUTE OF TECHNOLOGY

Volume 37 | Rochester, N.Y., Tuesday, November 21, 1961 | No. 8

An Editorial

A Challenge For Tomorrow

The Board of Trustees' decision of last night presents the students, alumni, faculty and administration with a very real challenge for tomorrow. The action the board has so courageously taken is unparalleled in its significance to RIT and the community it serves, and will be applauded by untold generations of students.

Motivated by the spirit of the founders of the Institute, and with bold and imaginative plans for the long-term solutions to its problems, RIT can and will achieve its goal.

The course is now set and a bright and exciting future is assured. Although we as students will not be here to attend classes on the new campus, we can take pride in the knowledge that we have been a part of the dynamic growth of RIT and can remain a strong contributing factor to all the tomorrows that lie ahead.

The Reporter congratulates the Board for a visionary decision which will strengthen RIT's position in the front rank of American colleges.

Board of Trustees OK's Move To New 1,000 Acre Campus

Will Start Building Within Two Years

A move by Rochester Institute of Technology to a new 1,000-acre campus site in the Town of Henrietta was voted by the Institute's 35-member Board of Trustees at a meeting held last night at the Rochester Club.

The decision by the Board, called by RIT President Dr. Mark Ellingson "the most significant single act in the 132-year history of the Institute," was the culmination of more than two years of study by RIT and was favored by the Board members over an alter-

(Top left) RIT Reporter, November 1961
(Top right) RIT President Mark Ellingson announces move to Henrietta, Veteran's Court, 1961
(Bottom left) Students prepare for motorcade to Henrietta campus, 1961
(Bottom right) Motorcade to Henrietta campus, 1961

Announcement of the move to Henrietta, Veteran's Court, 1961

Nathaniel Rochester Hall, ca. 1960s

Art students in Veteran's Court, ca. 1960s

Students file into RIT City Center, ca. 1960s

RIT President Mark Ellingson (left) on the Henrietta property, 1964

CONSTRUCTION

Alfred Davis, vice president of development, and members of the RIT Women's Council viewing Henrietta campus from the observation platform, ca. 1963

Arthur L. Stern, chairman of the Board of Trustees (left), and President Mark Ellingson look at proposed model of the new campus, ca. 1963

Initial grading, looking south, 1964

(Top left) Start of excavation for George Eastman Hall, 1964
(Top right) Entrance to observation platform off East River Road, 1965
(Bottom left) Frank Ritter Ice Arena and George H. Clark Gymnasium under construction, 1966
(Bottom right) George Eastman Hall under construction, 1966

View of campus, looking east, 1966

George Eastman Hall, looking north, 1967

Ann Hayes, staff member in Admissions and Records, poses in future lobby of George Eastman Hall, 1965

Student Alumni Union, looking northwest, ca. 1967

Wallace Library and Thomas Gosnell Hall, looking northwest, 1967

Construction workers in Wallace Library, with view of Liberal Arts Hall, ca. 1967

Northern side of George Eastman Hall and Frank E. Gannett Hall, ca. 1967

George H. Clark Gymnasium and Campus Center, looking east, 1967

Academic side of campus, looking southeast, ca. 1967

Main entrance before final grading, ca. 1967

Artist Josef Albers (left) and visitors with mural in George Eastman Hall, 1969

WELCOME HOME, Mar

RIT President Mark Ellingson (second from right) welcomed to his new office at George Eastman Hall by Board Chairman Arthur Stern (far right) and others, 1968

OPENING

(Left) Henrietta campus dedication ceremony, October 1968
(Right) Arthur Stern (left) and student John Gundrum lower the time capsule at dedication ceremony, 1968

(Top left) Visitors viewing printing apparatus, Frank E. Gannett Hall, 1969
(Top right) Visitors in science laboratory, Thomas Gosnell Hall, 1968
(Bottom left) Visitors viewing Edith Woodward Pool, Student Alumni Union, 1969
(Bottom right) Student Alumni Union Dedication, 1968

Dedication weekend tours, Student Alumni Union, 1968

Dedication weekend, Wallace Library, 1968

(Top left) Dedication weekend, Liberal Arts Hall, 1968
(Top right) Dorm room, ca. 1968
(Bottom left) Dedication weekend train, 1968
(Bottom right) Dedication weekend, Student Alumni Union, 1968

(Left) Student Ralph Cyr cuts ribbon at the dedication ceremony, Student Alumni Union, 1968
(Right) Entrance to Student Alumni Union, 1969

Ragnhild Langlet, *Blue and White Tapestry*, cafeteria, Student Alumni Union, 1969

Student relaxing in Eastman Kodak Quad, ca. 1969

Students await arrival of runners returning from 666-mile relay to inaugurate new athletic facilities, Albert J. and Carolie R. Simone Plaza, 1968

Relay team returns from Washington, D.C., to new campus, Albert J. and Carolie R. Simone Plaza, 1968

GROWTH

Albert Paley, *The Sentinel*, in the Albert J. and Carolie R. Simone Plaza, 2017

Main entrance, 2003

Main entrance, 1972

(Left) Light fixtures at main entrance, looking north, 1971
(Top right) Main entrance sign, looking southeast, 1971
(Bottom right) Parking in snow, 1976

(Top left) Main entrance sign, looking west, 2017
(Bottom left) Main entrance roadway, looking south, 2006
(Right) Students posing at main entrance, 1968

MUDTUG
ARE YOU READY
ΦΔΘ
BALLROOM + LATIN
DANCECLUB!
PI KAPPA PHI ΠΚΦ Men of Class
EQUESTRIAN RIT

Student Alumni Union, 2009

Spring Weekend parade, main entrance, 1969

(Left) Spring Weekend, Student Alumni Union, 1969
(Top right) Campus Connections, Student Alumni Union, 1992
(Bottom right) Edith Woodward Pool, Student Alumni Union, 1968

Fireside Lounge, Student Alumni Union, 1972

Jones Chapel, Schmitt Interfaith Center, 1992

(Left) The Quarter Mile, 2007
(Top right) Campus Center, 2010
(Bottom right) George Eastman Hall, 2004

The Quarter Mile, looking west, 2008

Bookstore addition, Student Alumni Union, 1984

Wallace Library, looking southwest, 1968

(Top) Reflections on Wallace Library, 1975   *(Bottom)* Sun on Liberal Arts Hall, 1975

Slope east of Wallace Library, with view of George Eastman Hall, 1975

Snowboarding by Wallace Library, 2009

D. H. S. Wehle, *RIT Bengal Tiger,* 2016

(Top) First floor of Wallace Library, 2017
(Bottom) Gordon Bleach, *sCRYPT* project, Wallace Library addition, 1991

Jose de Rivera, *Construction #105*, Infinity Quad, 2017

Infinity Quad, 1972

(Top) Infinity Quad and James E. Gleason Hall, ca. 1968
(Bottom) Infinity Quad and Thomas Gosnell Hall, 1971

(Top) Bruce and Nora James Atrium, Thomas Gosnell Hall, 2000
(Bottom) Larry Kirkland, *Principia*, in Thomas Gosnell Hall, 1998

Commencement, Infinity Quad, 1988

Infinity Quad, 1978

(Top left) Joseph Albers, brick mural, Thomas Gosnell Hall, 1979
(Bottom left) Infinity Quad, looking east, 2013
(Right) James E. Gleason Hall, 2017

Eastman Kodak Quad, 2017

Eastman Kodak Quad, 1970

(Top) Students sketching, Tojo Meditation Garden, 1981
(Bottom) Spring class, Eastman Kodak Quad, 1981

(Top) Redesign and construction, Eastman Kodak Quad, 2003
(Bottom) Fall class, Eastman Kodak Quad, 2003

Eastman Kodak Quad entrance, 2004

School of Design balloon project, Eastman Kodak Quad, 1981

(Top left) Garden adjacent to Bausch and Lomb Center, 2017
(Bottom left) Harry Bertoia, *Burst*, in Booth Hall Lobby, 2017
(Right) Bausch and Lomb Center, 2017

(Top left) Bevier Gallery, James E. Booth Hall, 2001
(Top right) Vignelli Center for Design Studies exhibition area, 2017
(Bottom left) University Gallery, 2017
(Bottom right) William Harris Gallery, Frank E. Gannett Hall, 2017

Construction, Magic Spell Studios, 2017

(Left) Chester F. Carlson Center for Imaging Science, 1990
(Top right) Skylights, James E. Booth Hall, 1974
(Bottom right) Walkway, James E. Booth Hall, 1972

Bausch and Lomb Center from Chester F. Carlson Center for Imaging Science roof, 1989

Vignelli Center for Design Studies

Juan Caballero-Perez and Leonard Urso, *Unity*, and Vignelli Center for Design Studies, 2017

West side, James E. Booth Hall, 1986

Construction, Center for Bioscience Education & Technology, 2005

Dedication of Engineering Technology Hall, 2007

(Top) James E. Gleason Hall, 2011
(Bottom) Interior, James E. Gleason Hall, 2009

(Top left) Engineering Hall, 2017
(Top right) Institute Hall, 2013
(Bottom left) Institute Hall and Center for Bioscience Education & Technology, 2017
(Bottom right) Golisano Hall, 2017

Unity Quad from north, 2013

Sustainability Institute Hall, 2017

(Left) Interior, Golisano Hall, 2017
(Top right) Golisano Hall, 2017
(Bottom right) Brick City Homecoming, Golisano Hall, 2009

Destler and Johnson Quad and Louise Slaughter Hall, 2017

Northwest side of campus, 2016

(Top left) Interior, Center for Bioscience Education & Technology, 2017
(Bottom left) Interior, Engineering Technology Hall, 2017
(Right) Interior, Sustainability Institute Hall, 2017

(Top left) Clinical Health Sciences Center, 2017
(Top right) Green roof, Sustainability Institute Hall, 2013
(Bottom left) Engineering Technology Hall, 2017
(Bottom right) Interior, Clinical Health Sciences Center, 2017

Albert Paley, *Cloaked Intentions*, in Destler and Johnson Quad, 2017

Campus, view from southwest, 2013

Residential Complex, Global Village Way, 2017

No Alcohol
Beyond
This Point

Global Village Plaza, 2017

(Left) Interior, Global Village 400 Suites, 2017
(Top right) Global Village Plaza and Student Innovation Hall, 2014
(Bottom right) Fountain Park, 2012

(Top) Thomas Gosnell Hall, south side, 2017
(Bottom) Max Lowenthal Hall, 2007

View of campus, looking northeast, 1979

View of campus, looking northwest, 1973

(Top) Interior, Max Lowenthal Hall, 1983
(Bottom) Henry Moore, *Three-Piece Reclining Figure*, outside of Max Lowenthal Hall, ca. 1980

(Top) Gene Polisseni Center, 2017
(Bottom) Construction, Gene Polisseni Center, 2014

(Top left) Young hockey fans, Frank Ritter Memorial Ice Arena, 2009
(Top right) Interior, Gene Polisseni Center, 2017
(Bottom left) Bike Path, 2011
(Bottom right) Turf field behind Wallace Library, 2016

Transit Plaza behind Wallace Library, 2017

Transit Plaza, looking southeast, 2013

Moonrise over dormitories, 1980

President Albert Simone (center) helps cut twenty-fifth anniversary cake, 1993

The Quarter Mile, Hale-Andrews Student Life Center, and August Center, 1993

(Top) Snow and tennis bubble, 1984
(Bottom) Tennis bubble deflation, 1992

The Quarter Mile in winter, ca. 1970

Gordon Field House and dormitories, 2013

(Top) RIT Pep Band on the steps of Gordon Field House, 2009
(Bottom) Track, Tiger Field, 2005

View of residence halls, looking northeast, 2013

Students in Sol Heumann Hall, looking west, 1970

(Top left) Dormitory courtyard, Residence Hall B, 1972
(Top right) Aleksandra Kasuba, Brick Mosaic, Sol Heumann Hall, 1972
(Bottom left) Gracie's dining hall, 1975
(Bottom right) Residence halls, 1975

(Top) Alistair Bevington, *Sundial*, Clocktower Quad, 1970
(Bottom) Construction, Central Quad, in front of Nathaniel Rochester Hall, 1972

(Top left) Alistair Bevington, *Sundial*, Clocktower Quad, 2014
(Top right) Orientation, East Quad, in front of Sol Heumann Hall, 2007
(Bottom left) Student murals in dormitory tunnels, 2008
(Bottom right) Helen Fish Hall, looking southeast, 2002

Construction, Lyndon Baines Johnson Hall, 1971

(Left) Frisina Quad, looking west, 1974
(Top right) The Commons, 1981
(Bottom right) Interior, Lyndon Baines Johnson Hall, 1974

Jan Strine Memorial Labyrinth, Frisina Quad, 2017

(Left) Interior, Lyndon Baines Johnson Hall, 2017
(Top right) Joseph F. and Helen C. Dyer Arts Center, Lyndon Baines Johnson Hall, 2001
(Bottom right) The Commons, 2006

(Top) Frisina Quad and CSD Student Development Center, 2006
(Bottom) Rosica Hall and Rosica DeCaro Meditation Garden, 2013

Carl Zollo, *Split Cube*, outside of Lyndon Baines Johnson Hall, 2017

RIT campus, looking northeast, 2013

PHOTO CREDITS

Every effort has been made to identify photographers. Unless otherwise noted, photos are courtesy of RIT Archive Collections.

xiv	B. Cook
5	University Archives and Special Collections, Paul V. Galvin Library, Illinois Institute of Technology
8 (left)	John Massey
8 (right)	Rodman S. Reilly
9	John Massey
19 (Top right)	Donald Smith
19 (Bottom right)	Freimark
20 (Top right)	Bill Barley
20 (Bottom left)	Bill Barley
20 (Bottom right)	Bill Barley
21	Bill Barley
29	Martin R. Wahl, Wahl's Photographic Service
31	Martin R. Wahl, Wahl's Photographic Service
56–57	Dawn and Bill DuBois
58	A. Sue Weisler
60 (Left)	John Massey
61 (Top left)	Dawn and Bill DuBois
61 (Bottom left)	Dave Londres
62–63	A. Sue Weisler
65 (Top right)	A. Sue Weisler
66	John Massey
68 (Left)	A. Sue Weisler
68 (Top right)	A. Sue Weisler
68 (Bottom right)	A. Sue Weisler
69	A. Sue Weisler
70–71	Jim Castelein
73 (Top)	B. Cook
73 (Bottom)	B. Cook
74	Doug Rea
75	Elizabeth Lamark
76	Elizabeth Lamark
77 (Top)	Dawn and Bill DuBois
77 (Bottom)	Gordon Bleach
78–79	Dawn and Bill DuBois
80	Jerry Zelada
81 (Bottom)	John Massey
82 (Top)	A. Sue Weisler
82 (Bottom)	A. Sue Weisler
83	Chris T. Quillen
85 (Bottom left)	Elizabeth Lamark
85 (Right)	Dawn and Bill DuBois
86–87	Dawn and Bill DuBois
89 (Top)	Nancy P. Legge
89 (Bottom)	Rodman S. Reilly
90 (Top)	A. Sue Weisler
90 (Bottom)	A. Sue Weisler
91	A. Sue Weisler
93 (Top left)	Dawn and Bill DuBois

93 (Bottom left)	Dawn and Bill DuBois
93 (Right)	Dawn and Bill DuBois
94 (Top left)	A. Sue Weisler
94 (Top right)	Dawn and Bill DuBois
94 (Bottom right)	Dawn and Bill DuBois
94 (Bottom left)	Dawn and Bill DuBois
95	Dawn and Bill DuBois
96 (Top right)	John Massey
96 (Bottom right)	Jerry Zelada
98–99	Dawn and Bill DuBois
100	John Massey
101	A. Sue Weisler
102	A. Sue Weisler
103 (Top)	Elizabeth Lamark
103 (Bottom)	Elizabeth Lamark
104 (Top left)	Dawn and Bill DuBois
104 (Top right)	Elizabeth Lamark
104 (Bottom left)	Dawn and Bill DuBois
104 (Bottom right)	Dawn and Bill DuBois
105	Elizabeth Lamark
106–107	Dawn and Bill DuBois
108 (Left)	Dawn and Bill DuBois
108 (Top right)	Dawn and Bill DuBois
108 (Bottom right)	A. Sue Weisler
109	Dawn and Bill DuBois
110	Elizabeth Lamark
111 (Top left)	Dawn and Bill DuBois
111 (Lower left)	Dawn and Bill DuBois
111 (Right)	Dawn and Bill DuBois
112 (Top left)	Dawn and Bill DuBois
112 (Top right)	Elizabeth Lamark
112 (Bottom left)	Dawn and Bill DuBois
112 (Bottom right)	Dawn and Bill DuBois
113	Dawn and Bill DuBois
114	Elizabeth Lamark
115	Dawn and Bill DuBois
116–117	Dawn and Bill DuBois
118 (Left)	Dawn and Bill DuBois
118 (Top right)	A. Sue Weisler
118 (Bottom right)	Elizabeth Lamark
119 (Top)	Dawn and Bill DuBois
119 (Bottom)	A. Sue Weisler

120–121	John Massey
122	Chris T. Quillen
123 (Top)	Rodman Reilly
124 (Top)	Dawn and Bill DuBois
124 (Bottom)	A. Sue Weisler
125 (Top left)	A. Sue Weisler
125 (Top right)	Dawn and Bill DuBois
125 (Bottom left)	Elizabeth Lamark
125 (Bottom right	Elizabeth Lamark
126	Dawn and Bill DuBois
127	Elizabeth Lamark
128–129	John Massey
130	A. Sue Weisler
131	A. Sue Weisler
132 (Top)	John Danicic
132 (Bottom)	A. Sue Weisler
134	Elizabeth Lamark
135 (Top)	Allie Ellis
135 (Bottom)	A. Sue Weisler
136–137	Elizabeth Lamark
139 (Top left)	Michael R. Soluri
139 (Bottom left)	Doug Rea
139 (Bottom right)	Andrew Franklin
140 (Bottom	Michael R. Soluri
141 (Top left)	A. Sue Weisler
141 (Top right	A. Sue Weisler
141 (Bottom left)	Elizabeth Lamark
141 (Bottom right)	A. Sue Weisler
143 (Left)	John Massey
143 (Top right)	Rodman Reilly
143 (Bottom right)	John Massey
144	Dawn and Bill DuBois
145 (Left)	Dawn and Bill DuBois
145 (Top right)	A. Sue Weisler
145 (Bottom right)	Ralph Smith
146 (Top)	Elizabeth Lamark
146 (Bottom)	A. Sue Weisler
147	Dawn and Bill DuBois
148–149	Elizabeth Lamark

INDEX

COLOPHON

Design

Marnie Soom

Production

True Creative

Typefaces

Helvetica Neue and Minion Pro

Paper

80# McCoy Silk

Printing and Binding

Jostens

This book was made possible, in part, through the support of the 50th Anniversary Committee.